IT'S TIME TO BAKE CHOCOLATE COOKIE CHEESECAKE

It's Time to Bake CHOCOLATE COOKIE CHEESECAKE

Walter the Educator

Silent King Books
A WhichHead Entertainment Imprint

Copyright © 2025 by Walter the Educator

All rights reserved. No part of this book may be reproduced in any manner whatsoever without written per- mission except in the case of brief quotations embodied in critical articles and reviews.

First Printing, 2025

Disclaimer

This book is a literary work; the story is not about specific persons, locations, situations, and/or circumstances unless mentioned in a historical context. Any resemblance to real persons, locations, situations, and/or circumstances is coincidental. This book is for entertainment and informational purposes only. The author and publisher offer this information without warranties expressed or implied. No matter the grounds, neither the author nor the publisher will be accountable for any losses, injuries, or other damages caused by the reader's use of this book. The use of this book acknowledges an understanding and acceptance of this disclaimer.

It's Time to Bake CHOCOLATE COOKIE CHEESECAKE is a collectible early learning book by Walter the Educator suitable for all ages belonging to Walter the Educator's Time to Bake Book Series. Collect more books at WaltertheEducator.com

USE THE EXTRA SPACE TO TAKE NOTES AND DOCUMENT YOUR MEMORIES

CHOCOLATE COOKIE CHEESECAKE

It's baking time, oh, what a treat,

It's Time to Bake Chocolate Cookie Cheesecake

Chocolate cookie cheesecake, so sweet!

Gather the goodies, let's get set,

This will be the best dessert yet!

First, we crush the cookies down,

Crunchy crumbs all nice and brown.

Mix with butter, soft and melted,

Our crust is ready, so well blended!

Pat the crust into a pan,

Smooth it out with your little hand.

Now we chill it, nice and cool,

This step makes our cheesecake rule!

Next comes cream cheese, silky and white,

Soft and fluffy, a creamy delight.

Add sugar, eggs, and vanilla,

Mix it together, it's starting to thrill ya!

It's Time to Bake Chocolate Cookie Cheesecake

Chocolate chips go in the mix,

Swirls of sweetness, give it a fix.

Stir it gently, fold it in,

This is where the fun begins!

Pour the batter on the crust,

Spread it even, that's a must.

Into the oven, warm and slow,

Our cheesecake bakes, a lovely glow.

While it bakes, we wait and dream,

Of chocolatey bites with a creamy gleam.

A little patience, just you see,

Soon it's time for a bakery spree!

Ding! It's ready, golden and fine,

The smell is heavenly, a tasty sign.

Let it cool, then chill it well,

It's Time to Bake Chocolate Cookie Cheesecake

The final flavor will surely excel.

Now for toppings, what should we do?

Whipped cream clouds or chocolate too?

Sprinkles, drizzles, or fruity flair,

Decorate it with love and care!

At last, it's ready, the big reveal,

Chocolate cookie cheesecake, a dreamy meal!

We'll slice and share, so much fun,

It's Time to Bake
Chocolate Cookie Cheesecake

Our baking adventure is second to none!

ABOUT THE CREATOR

Walter the Educator is one of the pseudonyms for Walter Anderson. Formally educated in Chemistry, Business, and Education, he is an educator, an author, a diverse entrepreneur, and he is the son of a disabled war veteran. "Walter the Educator" shares his time between educating and creating. He holds interests and owns several creative projects that entertain, enlighten, enhance, and educate, hoping to inspire and motivate you. Follow, find new works, and stay up to date with Walter the Educator™

at WaltertheEducator.com

www.ingramcontent.com/pod-product-compliance
Lightning Source LLC
LaVergne TN
LVHW052010060526
838201LV00059B/3944